COPYRIGHT PAGE

Copyright © 2023 By Dr. Lionel Rahn

For more information and free guidance contact author

dekine844@gmail.com

SCAN FOR MORE AUTHOR WORK

TABLE OF CONTENT

THE COMPLETE
LOW GLYCEMIC
FOOD LIST

MY PROVEN A-Z LIST OF
BLOOD GLUCOSE LEVEL FOODS

DR. LIONEL RAHN

INTRODUCTION

Food serves as our body's fuel. It provides us with energy, aids in body growth and repair, and promotes our general health and wellbeing. However, not all foods are made equally. Some meals have the potential to quickly raise blood sugar levels, which can result in conditions including diabetes, obesity, and heart disease.

Foods with a low glycemic index are healthier than those with a high glycemic index. Foods with a low glycemic index raise blood sugar levels gradually after consumption. This is as a result of their higher fiber content and slower rate of digestion.

A low-glycemic diet has several advantages. It can aid in enhancing blood sugar regulation, lowering weight growth, and reducing the risk of developing chronic illnesses like diabetes, heart disease, and stroke.

This book serves as a thorough reference for low-glycemic foods. It features a category-by-category list of low-glycemic foods, advice on selecting and cooking low-glycemic foods, a sample meal plan, and recipes.

This book is for you whether you're new to low-glycemic eating or are seeking for fresh concepts and recipes.

Here are a few more advantages of eating a low-glycemic diet:

* Improved energy levels. Consuming low-glycemic foods will give you a continuous supply of energy, which will help you feel less tired and have more energy overall.

* Decreased appetite. Foods with a low glycemic index can aid in lowering cravings for fatty and sugary foods. This is because they

aid in preventing spikes and crashes and helping to maintain steady blood sugar levels. Mood improvement and stress reduction are two benefits of low-glycemic meals. This is because they support blood sugar regulation and mood stabilization.

* Sleep better. Low-glycemic meals can improve your quality of sleep at night. This is due to the fact that they support stress reduction and a healthy blood sugar balance.

A low-glycemic diet is a fantastic choice if you want to eat in a healthier way. You will find all the knowledge you require in this book to begin going.

What is a low-glycemic diet?

Imagine eating a diet that makes you feel energized, full, and healthy. a diet that lowers your chance of chronic diseases while also assisting you in losing weight and improving blood sugar control. A low-glycemic diet is focused on achieving this.

A low-glycemic diet is an eating strategy that prioritizes foods with a low glycemic index (GI). How fast a food elevates blood sugar levels is determined by the GI. High GI foods generate a sharp rise in blood sugar followed by a slump. This may result in drowsiness, appetite, and desires for sweet foods.

On the other hand, foods with a low glycemic index raise blood sugar levels gradually. You will continue to feel energized and satisfied as a result throughout the day. Additionally, it aids in blood sugar control and lowers the risk of developing chronic illnesses including diabetes, heart disease, and stroke.

So how exactly does a low-glycemic diet function? The key is to make the appropriate food choices. Fruits, vegetables, whole grains,

and legumes all have low glycemic indexes. Because they include a lot of fiber and nutrients, these foods take longer for your body to digest. Your blood sugar levels will remain steady as a result of the slower release of glucose into your blood.

The following are some pointers for eating a low-glycemic diet:

* Pick fruits and vegetables with a low GI rating. For instance, low-GI foods include apples, berries, pears, and plums. Low-GI veggies include broccoli, cauliflower, spinach, and kale.

* Select whole grains instead than processed grains. Compared to refined grains, whole grains have a lower GI and are a rich source of fiber and minerals. For instance, whole-wheat bread and brown rice both have lower GIs than white rice and white bread, respectively.

* Be sure to eat some legumes. Beans, lentils, and peas are examples of legumes that are high in fiber, low in GI, and a rich source of protein.

* Consume less processed food and sugary beverages. High GI foods and beverages and processed foods can induce a sharp rise in blood sugar levels.

A low-glycemic diet is a healthy and sustainable method to improve your blood sugar control, decrease weight, and lower your chance of developing chronic diseases. It's a tasty way to eat, too! You're likely to find a diet that you can enjoy for the rest of your life with the wide variety of delectable low-GI items available.

Why is a low-glycemic diet beneficial?

Foods with a low glycemic index (GI) are the main emphasis of a low-glycemic diet. A food's GI value shows how quickly it boosts blood sugar levels. High GI foods generate a sharp blood sugar increase followed by a drop. Fatigue, hunger, and desires for sweet foods may result from this.

Contrarily, foods with a low glycemic index cause blood sugar levels to rise gradually. This makes you feel energized and full of satisfaction all day long. Additionally, it lowers your risk of developing chronic illnesses like diabetes, heart disease, and stroke and helps to control your blood sugar levels.

Here are just few of the numerous advantages of adhering to a low-glycemic diet:

- Blood sugar control improvement .
- Weight loss .
- Decreased risk of chronic diseases.
- Improvements in energy levels.

- Decreased cravings.
- Mood improvement.
- Sleep better.

A low-glycemic diet is a fantastic choice if you're seeking for a solution to enhance your general health and wellbeing. It provides a wealth of advantages and is a delectable and environmentally friendly way to eat.

How to use this book

This book is designed to be a comprehensive resource for anyone who is interested in following a low-glycemic diet. It shows detailed information on the following topics:

- What is a low-glycemic diet and why is it beneficial?
- A list of low-glycemic foods by category
- Tips for choosing and preparing low-glycemic foods
- A sample meal plan
- Recipes

To use this book, simply refer to the appropriate section for the information you

need. For example, if you are new to low-glycemic eating, you may want to start by reading the introduction and the chapter on tips for low-glycemic eating. If you are looking for a specific food, you can refer to the list of low-glycemic foods by category. And if you are looking for meal ideas, you can refer to the sample meal plan or the recipes.

Here are some additional tips for using this book:

- Keep it on hand in your kitchen so that you can refer to it when you are planning meals and snacks.
- Use it to create your own personalized low-glycemic meal plan.
- Mark your favorite recipes so that you can easily find them again.
- Share it with your friends and family so that they can learn about the benefits of a low-glycemic diet.

This book will help you to achieve your health and wellness goals.

CHAPTER 1

Low-glycemic Fruits And Vegetables

A healthy diet must include fruits and vegetables, which are also an excellent source of low-glycemic meals. Fruits and vegetables with a low glycemic index (GI) are known as low-glycemic foods. A food's GI value indicates how rapidly it boosts blood sugar levels. Low GI foods gradually raise blood sugar levels, which keeps you satiated and energized throughout the day.

According to some study, eating a diet high in low-glycemic fruits and vegetables may have several health advantages, such as:

*Weight reduction or maintain

* Better blood sugar management

* decreased chance of developing chronic illnesses such type 2 diabetes, heart disease, and stroke

Some low-glycemic fruits and vegetables are listed below:

Fruits

Apples, Cherries, Grapefruit, Oranges, Pears, Plums, Strawberries, Berries (blueberries, raspberries, strawberries, and blackberries), Pears, and Strawberries.

Vegetables

*Greens (spinach, kale, collard greens, Swiss chard)
* Artichokes * Asparagus * Broccoli
* Brussels sprouts * Cabbage * Carrots (raw)
* Cauliflower * Celery * Cucumbers

* Eggplant * Garlic * Mushrooms
* Onions * Peppers * Tomatoes

The maturity of the produce should be taken into account while selecting fruits and vegetables. Compared to unripe fruits and vegetables, ripe produce has a lower GI. Unripe bananas have a higher GI than ripe bananas, for instance.

Understanding the techniques used to prepare fruits and vegetables is also crucial. Some cooking techniques, such frying, can raise a food's GI. As an illustration, baked potatoes have a lower GI than fried potatoes.

The following advice will help you include low-glycemic fruits and vegetables in your diet:

Consume a variety of fruits and vegetables throughout the day; select ripe produce; and prepare food using techniques that don't raise the GI of the dish. Add fresh produce in your meals and snacks.

Here are some examples of low-glycemic fruits and vegetables you may include in your diet:

* Eat a bowl of oatmeal with berries and almonds to start your day.
* Include a side salad with your meal.
* Enjoy a hummus-topped snack of carrots or celery.
* Dinner will be a bowl of vegetable soup.
* Include some spinach in your smoothie in the morning.

Your general health and wellbeing will increase if you consume low-glycemic fruits and veggies.

Fruits: A-Z list of low-glycemic fruits

Apples: Apples are a traditional fruit that are high in fiber and low in calories. Additionally, they are a good source of potassium and vitamin C. Apples have a low GI of 39, which is regarded as average.

Berries: Berries are a fruit that tastes great, is healthy, and has a lot of antioxidants. In

addition, they provide a considerable amount of fiber and vitamin C. Berries have a considered low GI range of 25–53.

Cherries: Cherries are a delicious, juicy fruit that are strong in antioxidants and low in calories. In addition, they provide a considerable amount of fiber and vitamin C. The GI for cherries is 41, which is regarded as low.

Grapefruit: Citrus fruit grapefruit has a high vitamin C content and little calories. It is an excellent source of potassium and fiber as well. The GI for grapefruit is 25, which is regarded as low.

Oranges: Oranges are a citrus fruit that are high in vitamin C and low in calories. They are also an excellent source of potassium and fiber. The GI for oranges is 45, which is regarded as low.

Pears: Pears are a delicious, juicy fruit that are high in fiber and low in calories. Additionally, they are a good source of potassium and vitamin C. The GI of pears is 36, which is regarded as low.

Plums: Plums are a sweet, juicy fruit that are high in fiber and low in calories. Additionally, they are a good source of potassium and vitamin C. The GI for plums is 24, which is regarded as low.

Strawberries: Strawberry is a fruit that tastes great, is healthy, and has a lot of antioxidants. In addition, they provide a considerable amount of fiber and vitamin C. The GI for strawberries is 40, which is regarded as low.

Other low-glycemic fruits include:

* Kiwis.   * Lemons   * Limes
* Mangos   * Nectarines   * Passion fruit
* Peaches.   * Persimmons   * Pineapples
* Pomegranates * Prunes.   * Rhubarb
* Star fruit * Watermelon   * Apricots
* Avocados.   * Cantaloupe.   * Guava
* Honeydew melon

The maturity of the fruit should be taken into account while picking fruits. The GI of ripe fruits is lower than that of unripe ones. Unripe bananas have a higher GI than ripe bananas, for instance.

Understanding how fruits are prepared through cooking is also crucial. Some cooking techniques, such frying, can raise a food's GI. As an illustration, baked apples have a lower GI than fried apples.

The following advice will help you include low-glycemic fruits in your diet:

Eat a range of fruits throughout the day; select ripe fruits; prepare your food using techniques that don't raise its GI; and include fruits in your meals and snacks.

Here are some examples of low-glycemic fruits you may include in your diet:

* Eat a bowl of oatmeal with berries and almonds to start your day.
* Include some fresh fruit on the side with your breakfast or lunch.
* For a nutritious snack, make a fruit smoothie.
* To yogurt or cottage cheese, add fruit.
* Add some fruit to your salad.
* Serve fruit as a side dish after grilling it.

You will enhance your general health and wellbeing by including low-glycemic fruits in your diet.

Vegetables: A-Z list of low-glycemic vegetables

In the realm of food, vegetables are the unsung heroes. They're an important part of a healthy diet since they're full of minerals, antioxidants, and fiber. However, when it

comes to glycemic index (GI), not all veggies are made equal. How rapidly a food elevates blood sugar levels is determined by the GI. Vegetables with a GI of 55 or below are considered low-glycemic.

Following is an alphabetical list of low-glycemic vegetables:

Artichokes, asparagus, bell peppers, cabbage, raw carrots, cauliflower, celery, chicory, endive, escarole, fava beans, fennel, garlic, ginger, beets, broccoli, Brussels sprouts, bell peppers, carrots, and cabbage. (spinach, kale, collard greens, Swiss chard) * Green beans * Hearts of palm * Jerusalem artichokes * Kale * Leeks * Lettuce * Mushrooms * Mustard greens * Okra * Onions * Peas * Peppers * Potatoes * (sweet) * * Pumpkin *

Low-glycemic veggies are a fantastic method to increase your diet's nutritional, antioxidant, and fiber content without significantly

boosting your blood sugar levels. Additionally, they are adaptable and work well in a number of meals.

Following are some pointers for including low-glycemic veggies in your diet:
Choose fresh or frozen veggies; consume a variety of vegetables throughout the day; and prepare vegetables using healthy techniques like grilling, steaming, or baking. Eat more veggies during meals and snacks.

You may include low-glycemic veggies to your diet in the following ways:

* Have a bowl of spinach and mushroom-flavored porridge to start your day.
* Include a salad with your lunch.
* Have a hummus-and-carrots snack.
* For dinner, have a bowl of vegetable soup.
* Include some spinach in your morning smoothie.
   Your general health and wellbeing can be enhanced by include low-glycemic veggies in your diet.

Imagine yourself strolling through a lovely garden, surrounded by luxuriant green foliage and vibrantly colored produce. Ripe tomatoes' delicious perfume and the fragrant freshness of herbs fill the air. You pause to take in the sight of a head of broccoli with its closely spaced florets resembling a little forest. You select a spinach leaf and take a bite, relishing the somewhat bitter taste. With your eyes closed, you take a deep intake of the clean air and feel the sun on your skin and the breeze on your hair.

Eating low-glycemic veggies gives you this feeling. They are tasty, healthy, and freshly made. They are a great way to spice up your diet and provide variety, and they are also beneficial to your general health.

Pick up some low-glycemic veggies the next time you're at the grocery store. Don't expect to be let down.

Chapter 2

Low-glycemic whole grains and legumes

Legumes and whole grains are two of the world's most nutrient-dense dietary categories. They both include a lot of protein, fiber, and important vitamins and minerals. Additionally, both of them are low-glycemic, which results in a slow increase in blood sugar levels after eating.

They are therefore a fantastic option for persons with diabetes or other blood sugar management issues, as well as for those looking to drop some pounds or get healthier in general.

Complete grains

Oats, wheat, and rice are a few examples of plants whose seeds are whole grains. The bran, germ, and endosperm—the three components of the kernel—are all present in them. The most nutrient-dense components of the kernel are the bran and germ, which are also the ones that are eliminated when grains are refined.

Due to their greater starch and lower fiber content, refined grains have a higher GI than whole grains. A form of carbohydrate called starch is readily converted to sugar by the body.

In contrast, whole grains have a higher fiber content and a lower starch content. As a result, they digest more slowly and result in a more steady increase in blood sugar levels.

Here are some instances of whole grains with low glycemic index:

* Bulgur * Barley * Rye * Millet * Oats *

Quinoa * Brown * Wild * Rice * Whole-wheat

bread and spaghetti

Legumes

Beans, lentils, and peas are examples of plants of the legume family, and their seeds are known as legumes. They include important vitamins and minerals, fiber, and protein.

Legumes also have a low GI, which makes them a healthy option for persons with diabetes or other issues controlling their blood sugar.

Some examples of low-glycemic legumes are as follows:

* Edamame (soybeans) * Black beans * Kidney beans * Pinto beans * Garbanzo beans (chickpeas) * Lentils * Split peas

How to include whole grains and legumes with low glycemic index in your diet

Whole grains and legumes with low glycemic index can be included to your diet in a variety of ways. Here are some pointers:

*Eat a bowl of quinoa or porridge to start the day. * Include brown rice or wild rice in your meals.*
Opt for whole-wheat pasta and bread over white pasta and bread.
Add roasted chickpeas or edamame as a snack.
Include beans, lentils, or peas in your soups, stews, and salads.

Here are some illustrations of whole grains and legumes-based low-glycemic meals and snacks:

Breakfast options include oatmeal with berries and nuts, whole-wheat toast with avocado and eggs, yogurt parfait with quinoa and fruit. Lunch options include a salad with grilled salmon and chickpeas, lentil soup, and a whole-wheat wrap with black beans and vegetables. Dinner options include a quinoa stir-fry with chicken and vegetables, black bean burgers on whole-wheat buns, and lentil soup.

Snack options include roasted chickpeas,

You may enhance your general health and wellbeing by eating more low-glycemic whole grains and legumes. They are a wonderful and healthy way to spice up your meals and snacks and provide variety.

Let's now add a little bit of intrigue.

Consider yourself the chef of a renowned restaurant. Your clients travel from all over the world to sample your cuisine since it is

well recognized for its inventiveness and deliciousness.

One day, a brand-new patron enters your eatery. She is a young woman with diabetes who wants to eat something wholesome and delectable.

You cook her a dish with nutritious grains and legumes that have a low glycemic index. To begin, roast some chickpeas. The quinoa is then prepared and combined with the chickpeas. Olive oil and some grilled veggies are also added.

Your customer is thrilled when you offer her the food. It is the greatest supper she has eaten in a while, according to her.

Knowing that you enabled your client to have a tasty and nutritious lunch makes you happy.

Whole grains and legumes with low glycemic index are a versatile component that may be utilized to make a range of mouthwatering recipes. You may simply include them into your diet and enhance your general health and wellbeing with a little imagination.

Whole grains: A-Z list of low-glycemic whole grains

* Amaranth
* Barley
* Brown rice
* Buckwheat
* Bulgur
* Farro
* Freekeh
* Millet
* Oats
* Quinoa
* Rye
* Sorghum
* Spelt
* Teff
* Wild rice
* Whole-wheat

Whole grains with low glycemic index are a fantastic source of fiber, protein, and important vitamins and minerals. They are an excellent option for those who are attempting to lose weight or improve their general health

as well as those who have diabetes or other issues controlling their blood sugar.

The following advice will help you include low-glycemic whole grains in your diet:

* Eat a bowl of quinoa or porridge to start the day. * Include brown rice or wild rice in your meals.
* Opt for whole-wheat pasta and bread over white pasta and bread.
* To salads, soups, and stews, add whole grains.
* Popcorn or whole-grain crackers are good snacks.

Whole grains with a low glycemic index are a delicious and healthy way to spice up and diversify your diet. You may enhance your general health and wellbeing by include them in your meals and snacks.

Legumes: A-Z list of low-glycemic legumes

Here is an A-Z list of low-glycemic legumes:

* Adzuki beans
* Black beans
* Black-eyed peas
* Chickpeas (garbanzo beans)
* Cowpeas
* Fava beans
* Kidney beans
* Lentils
* Lima beans
* Mung beans
* Navy beans
* Pinto beans
* Split peas
* Soybeans (edamame)

Protein, fiber, and vital vitamins and minerals are all present in large quantities in legumes. They are an excellent option for those who are attempting to lose weight or improve their general health as well as those who have

diabetes or other issues controlling their blood sugar.

In many different meals, including soups, stews, salads, and burritos, legumes can be included. They may also be used to produce bread, pasta, and other baked foods by being pounded into flour.

The following advice will help you include low-glycemic legumes in your diet:

* Include beans in your soups, stews, and salads.
* Prepare a black bean burger or a lentil soup for lunch.
* Eat edamame or roasted chickpeas as a snack.
* Dress up your vegetables with hummus or bean dip.
* Create your own bread, pasta, and other baked foods with legume flour.

Low-glycemic beans are a tasty and healthy way to spice up and diversify your diet. You may enhance your general health and

wellbeing by including them in your meals and snacks.

Chapter 3

Low-glycemic dairy products and nuts

Two of the world's most nutrient-dense food categories are dairy and almonds. They both include a lot of protein, good fats, and vital vitamins and minerals. Additionally, both of them are low-glycemic, which results in a slow increase in blood sugar levels after eating.

They are therefore a fantastic option for persons with diabetes or other blood sugar management issues, as well as for those looking to drop some pounds or get healthier in general.

Lactose-free dairy products

Dairy products with a low GI have a slow effect on blood sugar levels after consumption, making them low-glycemic.

Here are some examples of dairy products with low glycemic index:

Kefir, cottage cheese, low-fat milk, Greek yogurt, and sour cream are all examples of dairy products.

Low-glycemic nut products

Nuts are an excellent source of protein, fiber, healthful fats, and important vitamins and minerals. They are also low-glycemic, making them a fantastic option for those who struggle to regulate their blood sugar due to diabetes or other conditions.

Here are a few low-glycemic nut examples:

Almonds, Brazil nuts, Cashews, Macadamias, Pecans, Pistachios, and Walnuts

How to include nuts and low-glycemic dairy products in your diet

Low-glycemic dairy foods and nuts can be incorporated in a variety of ways into your diet. Here are some pointers:

* Have a cup of Greek yogurt with berries and almonds to start your day.
* Include cottage cheese in your fruit or salad bowls.
* Eat a few nuts as snacks all day long.
* Your smoothies can be made with yogurt or low-fat milk.
* When making sandwiches and wraps, use low-fat cheese.

Following are some illustrations of low-glycemic meals and snacks that contain dairy and nuts:

Breakfast options include Greek yogurt with berries and nuts, cottage cheese with fruit, and whole-wheat toast. Lunch options include salads with grilled chicken and avocado, and dinner options include lentil soup with whole-wheat bread and salmon with roasted vegetables. Snack options include nuts, hard-boiled eggs, yogurt parfait with fruit, and granola.

Let's now add a little bit of intrigue.
Consider yourself a hiker on a difficult, lengthy journey. You've been hiking for hours and are becoming hungry and fatigued.

You take a break and have a snack. You take out a piece of fruit and a bag of almonds. When you bite into a nut, a burst of rich, creamy flavor fills your lips. The fruit's sweet, juicy flavor quenches your thirst as you bite into it. You start to feel more energized and prepared to carry on with your hike.

Nuts and dairy products with low glycemic indexes are excellent sources of energy and

satisfaction all day long. They are a filling and delectable snack that might assist you in achieving your fitness objectives.

Low-glycemic dairy foods and nuts are excellent choices for anybody aiming to live a healthy lifestyle, whether they are cyclists, hikers, or simply regular people.

Dairy products: A-Z list of low-glycemic dairy products

Here is an A-Z list of low-glycemic dairy products:

* Cottage cheese
* Feta cheese
* Goat cheese
* Greek yogurt
* Hard cheeses (cheddar, Swiss, Parmesan, etc.)
* Kefir
* Low-fat milk
* Low-fat yogurt

* Mozzarella cheese
* Ricotta cheese
* Skyr
* String cheese

Dairy products with a low glycemic index are a wonderful source of protein, calcium, and other necessary vitamins and minerals. They are an excellent option for those who are attempting to lose weight or improve their general health as well as those who have diabetes or other issues controlling their blood sugar.

It's crucial to choose low-glycemic dairy products by keeping an eye out for those that are low in fat and sugar. Additionally, it is crucial to select goods manufactured with whole milk as this will guarantee that they are an excellent source of nutrients.

The following advice will help you include low-glycemic dairy foods in your diet:

* To your salads or sandwiches, add cottage cheese, feta cheese, or goat cheese.
* For breakfast or lunch, enjoy a bowl of Greek yogurt with berries and almonds.
* Your smoothies can be made with yogurt or low-fat milk.
Make pizzas, wraps, and sandwiches using low-fat cheese. Grab a string cheese or hard cheese stick for a snack.

Dairy products with a low glycemic index are a tasty and healthy way to spice up and diversify your diet. You may enhance your general health and wellbeing by include them in your meals and snacks.

Nuts: A-Z list of low-glycemic nuts

A-Z list of low-glycemic nuts:

* Almonds
* Brazil nuts
* Cashews
* Hazelnuts
* Macadamia nuts
* Pecans
* Pistachios
* Walnuts

Nuts are a satisfying and healthy snack with a low glycemic index (GI). A food's GI value indicates how rapidly it elevates blood sugar levels after consumption. Low-GI meals raise blood sugar levels gradually, which is advantageous for those with diabetes or other issues with blood sugar regulation.

Additionally a wonderful supply of fiber, protein, and healthy fats are nuts. Additionally, they are rich in vitamins and minerals including vitamin E, magnesium, and potassium.

The following advice will help you include low-glycemic almonds in your diet:

* Snack on a handful of nuts throughout the day. * Include nuts in your salads, cereal, and yogurt.
* Spread nut butter on sandwiches and wraps.
* You may add nut milk to your coffee and smoothies.

Here are a few examples of delectable and wholesome snacks made using low-glycemic nuts:

Your favorite nuts, seeds, and dried fruit can be combined to make a trail mix. * Apple slices with almond butter: This traditional snack is scrumptious and wholesome.

A nutritious and filling snack is a yogurt parfait with nuts and berries.
* A sandwich with nut butter and banana is another option. This quick and simple snack is ideal for traveling.

Low-glycemic nuts are a tasty and healthy way to spice up and diversify your diet. They can assist you in maintaining your energy and satisfaction throughout the day.

Fun fact: Trees' seeds are found in nuts. They are a well-liked snack food since they are tasty, wholesome, and portable. Humans have consumed nuts for thousands of years.

This knowledge is intended to be useful. In case you have any other queries, just contact me.

Chapter 4

Low-glycemic recipes

We will delve into the realm of low-glycemic dishes in this chapter. Low-GI ingredients are those that are used in low-glycemic index (GI) recipes. The GI gauges how rapidly a meal elevates blood sugar levels after consumption. those with a low GI raise blood sugar levels gradually, whereas those with a high GI cause blood sugar levels to rise quickly.

People with diabetes or other blood sugar management issues, as well as those looking to drop a few pounds or get healthier overall, should go for low-glycemic dishes. They might also be a fantastic option for those who are only seeking for dishes that are healthier and more nourishing.

Low-glycemic dishes come in numerous varieties, ranging from breakfast to supper to snacks. Several instances include:

Breakfast options include whole-wheat bread, Greek yogurt with fruit and granola, cottage cheese with fruit, and oatmeal with berries and nuts.Lunch options include a salad with grilled chicken and avocado, a whole-wheat wrap with turkey and cheese, and lentil soup with whole-wheat bread. Dinner options include salmon with roasted veggies and quinoa and chicken stir-fry with brown rice.

Healthy cooking techniques including grilling, baking, and steaming should be used while preparing low-glycemic dishes. Additionally, it's crucial to stay away from processed meals and sugary beverages.

We will look at a selection of tasty and nourishing low-glycemic meals in the next chapters. Breakfast, lunch, supper, and snacks will all be included. Recipes for persons with unique dietary requirements, such as

vegetarians, vegans, and gluten-free diners, will also be included.

Here is a suggestion for creating your own low-glycemic dishes in the interim:

* Select ingredients that have a low GI to begin with. Use healthy cooking techniques like grilling, baking, and steaming. * Avoid using processed meals and sugary drinks. * Get inventive and experiment with various tastes and combinations.

You may easily come up with scrumptious and nourishing low-glycemic dishes that your entire family will love with a little imagination.

I'm hoping this chapter has whetted your appetite for low-glycemic food. We will examine a selection of scrumptious and nourishing meals that are guaranteed to delight everyone in the upcoming pages.

Low-Glycemic Breakfast recipes

Breakfast dishes with low glycemic index are a terrific way to start the day. They are created to support blood sugar regulation and maintain your level of energy throughout the morning.

Following are five delectable and healthy low-glycemic breakfast recipes:

1.Oats overnighted with nuts and berries

You may prepare this simple meal the night before to have a filling breakfast ready when you get up.

Ingredients:
1/4 cup yogurt, 1/4 cup berries, 1/2 cup rolled oats, 1/2 cup milk, and 1 tablespoon almonds.

Instructions:
1. In a jar, combine all the ingredients.
2. To blend, thoroughly stir.

3. Put the container in the fridge for the night.
4. Stir the oats in the morning and eat them.

2. Greek yogurt with fruit and granola, number two

Greek yogurt is low in fat and a fantastic source of calcium and protein. It creates a tasty and wholesome breakfast when combined with fruit and granola.

Ingredients:
Greek yogurt, one cup
* 1/4 cup granola * 1/2 cup fruit (such as berries, bananas, or thinly sliced apples)

Instructions:
1. In a bowl, combine all the ingredients.
2. To blend, thoroughly stir.
3. Enjoy!

3. Whole-Wheat Toast with Cottage Cheese and Fruit

Another excellent source of calcium and protein is cottage cheese. Additionally, it has less fat and sugar. It makes a tasty and filling breakfast when served with fruit and whole-wheat bread.

Ingredients:

* 1 piece of whole-wheat bread * 1/2 cup cottage cheese * 1/2 cup fruit (such as berries, bananas, or thinly sliced apples)

Instructions:

1. Top the whole-wheat bread with the cottage cheese.
2. Add fruit on top.
3. Enjoy!

4. A fruit, spinach, and yogurt smoothie

Get your recommended daily intake of fruits and veggies with smoothies. Additionally, making them is quick and simple. This smoothie has yogurt, spinach, and berries and is a fantastic source of vitamins, fiber, and protein.

Ingredients:

* One cup each of berries, spinach, yogurt, and milk.

Instructions:
1. Use a blender to combine all the items.
2. Purée until fluid.
3. Enjoy!

5. Hard-boiled eggs with avocado on whole-wheat toast

A interesting source of protein and good fats is hard-boiled eggs. They are a delightful and filling addition to whole-wheat bread and avocado for breakfast.

Ingredients:
1 slice of whole-wheat bread, 2 hard-boiled eggs, and 1/4 avocado

Instructions:
Eggs should be sliced and placed on whole-wheat bread.

2. Spread the mashed avocado over the eggs.
3. Enjoy!

Just a few examples of low-glycemic breakfast dishes are provided below. There are many of other mouthwatering and healthy choices available. You can easily make a breakfast that is both nutritious and filling with a little imagination.

I sincerely hope you enjoy and find these recipes useful.

* Low-Glycemic Lunch recipes

I understand the value of your lunch break as a working person. You need to eat in order to have the energy you need to go through the afternoon, but you don't have time to spend a lot of time in the kitchen doing it.

Low-glycemic lunch meals can help with that. Low-GI ingredients are those that are used in low-glycemic index (GI) recipes. The GI gauges how rapidly a meal elevates blood

sugar levels after consumption. those with a low GI raise blood sugar levels gradually, whereas those with a high GI cause blood sugar levels to rise quickly.

People with diabetes or other blood sugar management issues, as well as those looking to shed some pounds or improve their general health, should choose low-glycemic meals. They can also be a fantastic alternative for those who are just trying to find lunch options that are healthier and more nourishing.

Here are five tasty and healthy low-glycemic lunch meals that you can simply make ahead of time:

1. Quinoa salad with Mediterranean flavors

This salad's combination of quinoa, chickpeas, veggies, and herbs gives it a ton of flavor and nutrition. Additionally, it has a lot of protein and fiber, which will keep you full and content all afternoon.

Simply add cooked quinoa, chickpeas, finely chopped veggies, and your preferred herbs and spices in a dish to make this salad. Add a drizzle of lemon juice and olive oil, then season to taste.

2. Brown rice with Chicken Stir-Fry

A tasty and nutritious meal can be put on the table quickly and easily with this stir-fry. Additionally, it's a fantastic way to utilize leftover chicken or veggies.

Simply stir-fry your preferred veggies, cooked chicken, and preferred stir-fry sauce in a skillet to prepare this stir-fry. Over brown rice, please.

3. Lentil Soup

Low in calories and fat, lentil soup is a filling and substantial soup. Additionally, it has a lot of fiber and protein.

Simply put lentils, veggies, and broth in a saucepan and bring to a boil to make lentil soup. Reduce the heat, cover, and cook the lentils for a while. according to taste.

4. Whole-Wheat Bread Sandwich with Tuna Salad

Sandwiches with tuna salad are a traditional lunch choice for a reason. They are a fantastic source of protein and are quick and simple to prepare.

Simply combine some tuna with your preferred mayonnaise, celery, and onion, then spread the mixture over whole-wheat bread to create a tuna salad sandwich. To your tuna salad, you may also add more veggies like tomatoes, cucumbers, or carrots.

5. Fruit-and-Greek Yogurt Parfait with Granola

A delightful and healthful way to wrap your lunch is with this parfait. Additionally, it has plenty of calcium and protein.

Simply arrange Greek yogurt, fruit, and granola in a container or glass to create a parfait. Any fruit you choose, such as berries, bananas, or apples, can be used.

These are just a few illustrations of low-glycemic lunch ideas that are ideal for office workers. You may simply prepare your meals in advance with a little forethought so that you always have a filling lunch to enjoy.

Here are some more ideas for elevating the presentation of your low-glycemic lunches:

Include a variety of items in your lunch to help you feel energized and satiated throughout the afternoon. * Pack your lunch in a reusable container. This will help you save money and prevent trash.

Make sure your lunch looks appetizing. Make sure your meal looks beautiful because we consume food with our eyes first. Try presenting your meal in a unique and exciting

style, or add a garnish like a lemon slice or a bunch of parsley.

* Go on a lunch break. It's crucial to take a lunch break from work in order to refresh. Try to locate a peaceful area where you may unwind and relish your food.

These suggestions can help you make it simple to prepare and savor excellent, low-glycemic meals that are ideal for working people.

Low-Glycemic Dinner Recipes

1. Salmon with Quinoa and Roasted Vegetables

This recipe is loaded with nutrition and taste, and it's very simple to make. The veggies are roasted until they are fork-tender and caramelized, and the salmon is roasted until it is just right. The addition of some protein and

fiber from the quinoa transforms the dish into a full meal.

Ingredients:

1 cup chopped veggies (such broccoli, Brussels sprouts, carrots, or potatoes), 1 tablespoon olive oil, 1/2 teaspoon salt, 1/4 teaspoon black pepper, 1 salmon fillet (approximately 6 ounces), and 1/2 cup cooked quinoa.

Instructions:

1. Set the oven to 400 degrees Fahrenheit (200 degrees Celsius).

2. Arrange the salmon fillet on a parchment-lined baking pan.

3. Add salt and pepper and drizzle with olive oil.

4. Roast the salmon for 12 to 15 minutes, or until it is well done.

5. Roast the veggies on a different oven sheet for 20 to 25 minutes, or until they are soft and caramelized, while the salmon is cooking.

6. Arrange the fish and veggies on individual plates before serving.

7. Add quinoa on top, then relish!

2. Brown rice with Chicken Stir-Fry

This stir-fry is a quick and simple way to provide a tasty and healthy meal. Additionally, it's a fantastic way to utilize leftover chicken or veggies.

Ingredients:

1 cup chopped veggies (such as broccoli, bell peppers, onions, or carrots) * 1 tablespoon olive oil * 1 pound boneless, skinless chicken breasts * 1/4 cup stir-fry sauce * 1 cup cooked brown rice

Instructions:

1. In a big skillet or wok, heat the olive oil over medium-high heat.
2. Include the chicken and heat it until it is evenly browned.
3. Stir in the veggies, then simmer until they are soft.
4. Add the stir-fry sauce and heat it well.

5. Place on top of brown rice and savor!

3.Quinoa stuffed Bell peppers

Ingredients for quinoa-stuffed bell peppers: 4 big bell peppers of any hue

- 1 cup cooked quinoa - 1 cup rinsed and drained black beans
- 1/2 cup chopped onion - 1/2 cup corn kernels
- 1 cup diced tomatoes - 1 cup diced zucchini
- 1 teaspoon each of cumin and chili powder
- To taste-selected salt and pepper - Optional toppings: cheese, avocado, and cilantro

Instructions:
1. Set the oven temperature to 375°F (190°C).
2. Remove the bell peppers' tops and scoop out the seeds and white membrane.
3. Combine the black beans, diced tomatoes, zucchini, onion, corn kernels, cumin, chili powder, salt, and pepper in a dish with the cooked quinoa. To blend, thoroughly stir.
4. Place the bell peppers on a baking sheet and fill them with the quinoa mixture.

5. Bake for 25 to 30 minutes, or until the filling is well cooked and the peppers are soft.
6. Serve hot with extras like cilantro, avocado, and shredded cheese.

4. Turkey Lettuce Wraps:
Ingredients:
- 1 pound ground turkey
- 1 tablespoon olive oil
- 2 cloves garlic, minced
- 1 small onion, diced
- 1/2 cup diced bell peppers (any color)
- 1/2 cup grated carrots
- 2 tablespoons low-sodium soy sauce or tamari
- 1 tablespoon hoisin sauce
- 1 teaspoon sesame oil
- Salt and pepper to taste
- 8 large lettuce leaves (such as iceberg or butter lettuce)

Instructions:

1. Heat olive oil in a large skillet over medium heat. Add the ground turkey and cook until browned, breaking it up with a spoon.

2. Add the garlic, onion, bell peppers, and grated carrots to the skillet. Cook for a few minutes until the vegetables are softened.

3. In a small bowl, whisk together the soy sauce, hoisin sauce, sesame oil, salt, and pepper. Pour the sauce over the turkey mixture and stir well to combine.

4. Simmer for another 5 minutes to let the flavors blend together.

5. Spoon the turkey mixture onto the lettuce leaves, roll them up tightly, and secure with toothpicks if needed.

6. Serve the turkey lettuce wraps as a delicious and low-glycemic dinner option.

Low-Glycemic Snack Recipes

Here are five quick and delectable low-glycemic snack dishes that you can prepare in a matter of minutes:

1. Hard-boiled eggs: There is a reason why hard-boiled eggs are a traditional snack. They are low in calories and carbs and high in protein and good fats. Simply arrange the eggs in a single layer in a pot and cover with cold water to cook them hard. Once the water has reached a rolling boil, turn off the heat and cover the pan. For medium-cooked eggs, leave the eggs in the boiling water for 10 minutes; for hard-cooked eggs, leave them in for 12 minutes. Once the eggs are cool to the touch, drain the hot water and cover them with cold water. Enjoy the eggs after peeling them!

2. Trail mix: A nutrient-rich on-the-go snack, trail mix is fantastic. Additionally, it is a good source of fiber and protein. Simply add your preferred nuts, seeds, and dried fruit in a basin to create trail mix. Almonds, walnuts, pecans, sunflower seeds, pumpkin seeds, raisins, cranberries, and blueberries are a few of the most well-liked components. You may also use other ingredients like coconut flakes or dark chocolate chips.

3. Apple slices with peanut butter A traditional snack that is tasty and healthy is apple slices with peanut butter. Apples are an excellent amount of fiber and vitamins, while peanut butter is a fantastic supply of protein and beneficial fats. Simply slice an apple and put peanut butter over the pieces to make this snack. Additionally, you can use extra garnishes like cinnamon, honey, or raisins.

4. Cottage cheese with fruit and nuts: Calcium and protein are both abundant in cottage cheese. Additionally, it has less calories and carbs. Simply mix cottage cheese, fruit, and almonds in a dish to make this snack. Berries, bananas, and peaches are a few of the widely consumed fruits. Almonds, walnuts, and pecans are a few of the most consumed nuts. You may also use other ingredients like honey or cinnamon.

5. Yogurt parfait with fruit and granola: Yogurt parfaits are a tasty and nutritious treat that are a rich source of calcium and protein. Simply arrange yogurt, fruit, and granola in a

container or glass to create a yogurt parfait. You may use whatever kind of yogurt you prefer, including plain yogurt, Greek yogurt, and flavored yogurt. Berries, bananas, and apples are a few common fruits. Oat granola, nut granola, and seed granola are a few of the most well-liked varieties. You may also use other ingredients like honey or cinnamon.

These are just a few suggestions for quick and scrumptious low-glycemic snacks. You may simply make snacks that are ideal for your requirements and dietary restrictions with a little imagination.

Conclusion

The information in this book should be helpful to you in learning about the advantages of a low-glycemic diet and how to include low-glycemic items in your meals and snacks.

A low-glycemic diet can aid in better blood sugar management, lower the risk of heart disease, encourage weight reduction or management, boost energy levels, and enhance mood and cognitive performance.
I advise you to try eating a low-glycemic diet if you want to increase your general health and wellbeing. You may discover a diet that works for you because there are so many scrumptious and nourishing low-glycemic items available.

I appreciate you taking an interest in this subject, and I wish you continued success in your quest for a nutritious and balanced diet. Please don't hesitate to get in touch with me if you have any inquiries or comments.

Thank you once more for reading.

The Communication   Compass

Navigating Human Behavior in Business and Beyond

Nora S.Radley